VANITY UNFAIR

Vanity Unfair and Other Poems
© Robert Eugene Rubino / Cathexis Northwest Press

No part of this book may be reproduced without written permission
of the publisher or author, except in reviews and articles.

First Printing: 2022

Paperback ISBN: 978-1-962869-64-8

Design and Editing by C. M. Tollefson

Cathexis Northwest Press

cathexisnorthwestpress.com

VANITY UNFAIR

and other poems
by Robert Eugene Rubino

Cathexis Northwest Press

In memory of Gene & Jo

I'm grateful for family, friends, fellow writers and editors for their invaluable encouragement through the years, among them: Kenneth and Belinda Rubino; Donald Rubino and Larry Buckman; Tom Goldstein; Rich Mellott; Lowell Cohn; Stacey Swann; Rachel Howard; Donna Talarico; Ruben Quesada; Joshua Rivkin and the No Fear poets (George Lister, JoAnne Tillemans, Rebecca Dougherty, Jennifer Trainor and Michael Wachter) of Stanford Continuing Studies; Samuel Griffin; Sandra Squire Fluck; Clare MacQueen; Mary Pitman Kitch; Henry Stanton; Susan Warren Utley and Savannah Spidalieri; Guy Biederman; Tony Aldarondo; Dan Brady; Nazelah Jameson; Lisa Rosenberg; Monica Korde; C.M. Tollefson; and Sandra Anfang.

And of course extra loving gratitude to my wife, Terry Jacobs.

— Robert Eugene Rubino
June 2022
Palo Alto, California

Table of Contents

King for a Day	17
DNA Samples	19
Love in the Time of the Cuban Missile Crisis	20
Uncool Kid	21
Stickball Hallucination, 1958	22
Do-Overs	23
War on Poverty	24
Wrestling vs. Boxing	25
Yahweh in High School (1961-1965)	26
Muscle-Bound Hairy-Chested He-Man Crybaby	27
Here Lies Their Father Who Left	28
Wallflowers of the World, Unite!	29
A Septuagenarian Atheist Prays	30
Break Time	31
Security Guard Working Graveyard Shift at Your Memory Museum	32
Bootstraps	33
Wannabe Handyman	34
Rumble, Old Man, Rumble	35
Vanity Unfair	36
Hush, Memory	37
Will the Real You Please Stand Up	38
Nor Was He The Marlboro Man	39
Accident on the L.I.E.	40
Splish-Splash	42
Giving Thanks to Your Trash Collectors	44
What We Talk About When We Talk About Coffee	46
Clocks Striking Thirteen on a Bright Cold Day	48
Forgiven	49
Dreaming & Dancing	50
Poking Sharp Stick Into Insidious Eye — It's About Time	51
Mourning Doves & Morning Gunshots	54
Last Love Last	56
A Kiss at the Corner of 19th & Holloway	57
Reflections & Refractions at Bodega Bay	58
Facelift	59
Unhappily Happy	60
UFO Abduction	61
Arrow Stuck in Neck	62

Crawlspace	63
On Either Side of Broad Bay Window	64
Owl House	65
When Dying Deer Appeared	66
Burning Coals & Hothouse Flowers	67
Road to Recovery	68
Mother Knew Best	69
Catawampus	70
Best Friends & Devoted Lovers	71
Fact Checker's Notes (1996)	73
Postgame Wrap	75
Unsolicited Advice to the Sorrow-Stricken	76
Supremacy	78
Bone Marrow Biopsy Reverberations	79

King for a Day

Checkers pieces get reset yet again.
It's only a friendly game after all, right?
Right. As if we ever played any game
not wanting to annihilate the other.
He calmly assumes air of dignity

while hunched in a wheelchair
his chin looking like it's attached
to plaid shirt's buttoned top button
his oversized diaper bulging
over coffee-stained red sweatpants

his wrinkle-rutted face
splotched with dried blood
result of nursing-home aide's shave
his breath a labor of longing
watery eyes searching for land

his World War II combat brothers all gone
one just last week, now he's the last
his Josie, wife of 62 years, dead three months
family expects him to follow any day now
family will be wrong — by five years.

He makes yet another unruly triple jump
using whatever damn pieces
moving in whatever damn direction
he damn well pleases, this time adding
a flourishing finishing flick of his wrist

and guttural gargle of a command:
King me!
Well, I know a con job when I see it
or at least I think I do.
Hell, I really have no idea...

I sit & stare, shrug & sigh
no more resetting of pieces.
Time & toil crown my father
his tender tenor rasps & gasps:
Give up, wise guy?

DNA Samples

Your mother, a New York tenement child of the Great Depression & high school graduate
who was 19 when her mother died in her arms at 50...
Your father, a child of the Great Depression in the same tenement but a high school dropout
— a deez-dem-doze kind of guy who saw friends fellow soldiers die blown apart on Luzon...

your mother who became substitute mother for her brother eight years younger
& whose firstborn would one day follow his uncle & live out West
— adventures for them, abandonments for her...
your father who emerged from that so-called Good War with shrapnel-shrouded vision
& valiantly tried to board postwar America's working-class prosperity train...

your mother who soothed & sheltered her stroke-stricken father in his final years
& started & sustained a mid-life civil service career out of necessity absent any ambition...
your father whose Franciscan kindness softened the brattiest brats & beastliest beasts
& whose Ben Franklin-like common sense & sense of fair play beat back, usually, bunk & bias
— his own included...

your mother whose faith was defeated but not destroyed by the Church's sex-abuse scandals...
your father who never failed to volunteer for family duty no matter how fraught & fought
for family unity with the energy & determination of a Matterhorn mountaineer...

your mother who beat lymphoma & melanoma but not multiple myeloma...
your father whose ocean-swimming athleticism devolved into seizures-induced incontinence
& immobility...

your mother with coal-dark Irish eyes & sardonic wit until her last *whooshing* exhale at 87...
your father with espresso-dark Italian eyes & operatic emotions until his sigh of surrender at 93...

your mother & father held close to their hearts philosophies lived & breathed & handed down:
Don't complain. Things could be far worse — indeed will likely get far worse.
Instead, be kind. Be helpful. Be grateful.
And
Don't
Complain.

Love in the Time
of the Cuban Missile Crisis

An hour after our idolized lionized Catholic president tells the nation
any day now we might all get blown to Kingdom Come
you exit your parents' warmly lit living room
& step all bundled up into a windless chill of a mid-October starry night
a zit-faced skinny-as-a-stickball bat 14-year-old looking for the exotic
16-year-old non-Catholic girl next door walking her pint-sized full-sized dog
— with nuclear annihilation imminent you figure
you might as well bare your soul & tell her how you feel.

For nearly two weeks Kennedy & Khrushchev & Cuba
hold civilized existence in a chokehold of existential crisis
as lines into churches of all denominations spill out onto the streets
and for nearly two weeks on cold clear starry nights you find comfort
walking with the exotic girl next door & talking as if in a fever about
doomsday desires until like roiling wintry clouds crisis & fever pass
— the crisis with a collective exhaustive extended exhale
— the fever with a small surgical scar on your fragile still-forming psyche...

and an even smaller dog bite on your adolescent ass.

Uncool Kid

Were you at Shea Stadium in 1964
when you were sixteen
when you were living right there in Queens
when the Beatles
made their historic histrionic U.S.A. debut?

Yes, you were at Shea in '64! Yes you were!
...but it was to see the Mets-Giants Memorial Day doubleheader with your dad
and the second game lasted twenty-three innings
— more than seven hours
and you & your dad stayed for all of it!
Loved all of it!
Never got bored
not for a minute.
Never thought of leaving
not for a second.
Loved all of it.
Every run-hit-&-error of it.
Loved all of it!
Every crowd-thinning seat upgrade of it.
Every hot-dog eatin'
soda-pop slurpin'
Cracker Jack munching
& peanut shell spittin' bit of it!

People said it wasn't as cool as
seeing the Beatles.
They still say it.
You said it was way cooler than the Beatles.

And ... You still say it.

Was that heaven?
No. It was just father & son
spending all day all night watching ballgames in Queens in 1964
bonding like nothing else quite could ... or ever did ...

Was that heaven? Well, it sure as hell wasn't Iowa.
Hell, yeah, that was heaven.

Stickball Hallucination, 1958

Narrow car-crowded streets
tamed under Idlewild's cacophonous skies
became the wide-open cheer-splashed spaces
of old Yankee Stadium a borough away in the Bronx.

Sawed-off broomstick in your bony hands
became big-barreled Louisville Slugger
& ten-year-old skin-and-bones zero you
became Superman in pinstripes No. 7 muscular Mickey Mantle.

Pink rubber *Spaldeen* ball
became official big-league rock-hard hardball
its perfectly stitched horsehide soaring streaking like a comet's tail
into the upper reaches of the upper deck's facade of crowns.

Do-Overs (And So What If It's Fifty-Sixty Years Later?)

This time making father-pleasing game-winning catch & throw
instead of cringe-inducing game-losing error on rocky Little League sandlot
within noggin-gnashing noise of LaGuardia's arrivals & departures.

This time hitting nothing but net — swish! —
instead of shooting mind-of-its-own air ball
at junior varsity tryout in jocks-socks-sweat-smell gymnasium.

This time emoting lines like a white Paul Robeson
instead of stuttering stammering in school play
plagued by tongue-tied stage fright.

This time standing up to playground bully
instead of bowing head backing down
peered at pitied like lab slab specimen by whole world it seemed

— including kid brother who'd idolized you
— including first-ever girlfriend who'd soon become first ex-girlfriend.
This time? This time things will be different. Oh, yeah.

War on Poverty

One mother plus one father equal two parents.
Oldest brother plus middle brother plus baby brother equal three kids.
Two parents plus three kids equal family of five circa 1955.

One 9x12 living room plus one 12x15 kitchen/dining area plus one bunkbed to help squeeze
brothers into one 9x12 bedroom equal second-floor three-room apartment with radiator's hissing
heat in winter & no a.c. in summer in the city within earsplitting earshot of LaGuardia Airport.

Living room with couch that converts to bed for parents at night
equal second bedroom minus living room. Paper-thin wallpapered walls
divided by doors stuck ajar multiplied by whispered voices fail to equal privacy.

One toilet plus one sink plus one bathtub in 6x9 space equal one bathroom
whose light switched on in middle of the night scares & scatters
countless cockroaches — a.k.a. water bugs — conservative estimate: 20 on any given night.

This family of five has its own version of clown-car-crowding gag
cramming grandparents, uncles, aunts, neighbors, friends in three-room apartment
for holiday feasts, birthday bashes, graduation galas & no-particular-reason get-togethers.

Add vision of tinseled ceiling-scraping tree and tons of toys including bicycles at Christmas
— a vision every bit as miraculous as Bernadette's at Lourdes. None of it adds up to poverty, not
real poverty, not even a vague feeling of being poor — another miracle perhaps? No doubt.

Thanks to loans & lay-away plans & parental selflessness, bills get paid: orthodontics, speech
therapists, Catholic school, Catskill vacations, trips to Manhattan for culture & ballgames.
Father runs freight elevator. Mother gets telemarketing gig. Oldest son delivers newspapers.

Finally, four bedroom house in the suburbs of 1960 adds space the final frontier
for backyard barbecues plus space for privacy equaling neither happiness nor unhappiness
but multiplied stress fractures: grief & illness stress plus commuter & hormonal stress,
plus financial, familial, societal, even political stress.

Can't blame the 'burbs. Same fractures could've factored in the city. Indeed they do when
family returns humbled if not humiliated three years later. No, don't blame the 'burbs.
Blame timing. Or time. Or the times. They were a-changing, so it's been sung.

Wrestling vs. Boxing

It's false, it's fake, it's fantasy, it's scripted, it's silliness & at 14 I can't look away.
Musclebound bound-for-glory Bruno Sammartino getting set to pin villainous Killer Kowalski
to the mat, golden-maned Nature Boy Buddy Rogers sneaking up from behind & clobbering
Bruno with a folding chair, cueing 601-pound Haystack Calhoun to come to the rescue.
A magnificent melee ensues while the see-no-evil referee becomes an incurious bystander.

In my pliable Play-Doh of a mind, pro rasslin' via our 12-inch black & white TV in 1962
was violence stylized, violence operatic, violence as theater of the absurd
with ample amounts of huffing & puffing & blowing the house down
with headlocks & dropkicks & body slams & back-breakers & skull crushers & sleeper holds.
Violence at its best because nobody got hurt — they'd all be back next week — good as new.

Of course the attraction was made stronger by the revulsion expressed by my blue-collar father
— well-muscled himself — whose bellowing "It's phony, it's staged!" cued my cry of resistance:
"Oh yeah? Mr. America's bashed head bled last week. Real blood!" — even though I knew
it's all fake, even the blood, but that wasn't the point, the point being we watched stuff together
while eating thick-crust pizza — my rasslin' on Thursday nights, his Friday night fights.

I'd soak up his punchy boxing history lectures about the Great John L. & Gentleman Jim
& the Jacks — Johnson & Dempsey — & Joe Louis, of course, while mesmerized by
the sweet-science artistry of aging Sugar Ray Robinson or one-eyed courage of Carmen Basilio
but neither of us was prepared for the finale in the Emile Griffith/Benny 'Kid' Paret trilogy,
Griffith beating Paret to death after Paret called Griffith a faggot earlier that day at the weigh-in.

Griffith punching Paret in the head twenty-five times in the thirteenth round,
Paret giving nothing in return, Paret slumping but still on his feet, the ropes holding him up
but he's already gone, gone to where a K.O.'s black lights never blink, past the point of no return
while referee Ruby Goldstein stares at this public execution as if he's merely a curious bystander.
It's true, it's serious, it's unscripted, it's brutality, it's reality & at 14 I can't look away.

Yahweh in High School (1961-1965)

I.

We nicknamed him Yahweh
because the celibate young-buck
black-robed principal
of our all-boys Catholic high school
loomed like a crazy-scary-angry
Old Testament deity
whether raging against masturbation
(euphemistically called self-abuse)
or dispensing tough-love law & order
with a fist to the sternum
or knee to the scrotum
or hard-pressed knuckles
to the top of the skull
or ritualistic butt-baring paddling
with a paddle that looked like an oar
from the wreck of the Hesperus.

II.

As we survivors of our all-boys
Catholic high school lock-stepped
to off-key notes of Pomp & Circumstance
& endured a grueling gray graduation day
steeped in pledge-of-allegiance speeches
from our principal nicknamed Yahweh
condemning racial integration & godless communism
while beseeching the son of god's virgin mother,

a round red-faced fussy fusty yellow-vested boy
who for four years absorbed loneliness & laconic innuendo
like a true believing saintly stoic Crusader —
graduated to eternity by stepping off the Queensboro Bridge
— a sound bite of news that an eon before social media
still spread among us his classmates
as swiftly as an abandoned ugly urban lot set ablaze
by careless kids stubbornly striking not-so soggy matches.

Muscle-Bound Hairy-Chested He-Man Crybaby

Seven-year-old snaps
out of untroubled top-bunk sleep
awakened by awfully familiar but awfully off-key *basso profundo*
coming through thin wall from next room of three-room Queens apartment circa 1955.
Takes a moment for kid's audio night light to reveal
— can it be? is it possible? —
muscle-bound hairy-chested he-man father crying, no — sobbing,
can't-catch-his-breath sobbing shaking shivering with shame
laid off from night shift hat factory in lower Manhattan
a job that — in the kid's mind anyway —
had smelled of nasty nebulous embarrassment
akin to body odor.

Six-months-pregnant wife / mother
tries to soothe & settle husband / father
this manly man turned crybaby
this man of operatic emotions
at times tender & unembarrassed
with barely restrained bear hugs of primal protection
at other times with eye-blink-quick anger
launching ladle-full of mashed potatoes
into flying saucer of spuds
slung from stove to kitchen's wallpapered walls
— splat! —
a sound resounding with unsightliness.

Father's sobbing
soon-but-not-soon-enough
subsides
but much nastier more nebulous
illiterate bare-ass embarrassment
takes root
plunging deep down deep
into seven-year-old's now-troubled top-bunk sleep.

Here Lies Their Father Who Left

They remember him
through a gauzy backward glance
a decent dad — decent enough, anyway:

funny & sad
smart & stupid
hardworking & lazy
generous & cheap
goofy & morose
corny & profound
sensitive & insensitive
strong & weak
selfish & selfless
righteous & wrong-headed.

Loving?
Sure — as far as it went.

They remember him (with gauze removed)
as vividly as a sinkhole
sucking down their home's foundation
their father who left their mother
their suddenly sad mad mother
interrupting their dully addictive watching
of their daily family comedy-drama.

They remember him
leaving but don't remember his reasons
never gave a good goddamn about his reasons.

They remember
the father who left them
—his sons, ages 18 & 13 —
sure, he didn't go far & always made himself available
—as far as that went — but still...
he left them
with their forever sad mad mother.

They remember him.

Wallflowers of the World, Unite!

We Baby Boomer wallflowers
having barely begun our body blooming years
mere months since first menstruation first erection

must have looked like bug-eyed fungus
our backs against the world against a wall
of a nearly finished suburban basement

as if in a Twilight Zone police lineup
suspected of doing nothing (or next to nothing)
too afraid to follow the new normal's hormonal urges

as our hipper cooler hotter braver better-complexioned peers
slow-as-molasses slow-danced to Johnny Mathis songs
before graduating to frisky French kissing

on couches demoted from the plastic-coated living room upstairs
where Greatest Generation parents consoled themselves
by staring at their state-of-the-art color TV console

flipping from Nixon-Kennedy speechifying
to Jackie Gleason playing spousal abuse for laughs
and smoke-and-mirrors ads sexualizing nicotine addiction.

As aromas of perfume
more like fresh-baked sugar-glazed peach pie
wafted from newly breasted girls-becoming-women

as aromas of cologne
more like spilled tumblers of Christian Brothers brandy
wafted from first-time shaved boys-becoming-men

as one wallflower's politely ruthless rejection
of another's painfully belated dance offer
somehow certified all our freshly minted guilty innocence

we wallflowers silently stared into our geeky grim here-and-now
desperate for a time machine (or merely better timing)
as the misty music lingered in the subterranean air.

A Septuagenarian Atheist Prays

I.

Breathe in
hold breath
breathe out
deepen breath
deepen life
melt ego

find kindness
lose anger
lick wounds
count blessings
jump for joy
sit with sorrow

foster hope
stand for peace
reach for empathy
strive for civility
laugh freely
free from sarcasm

always forgiving
hale and hearty
breathe out
hold breath
breathe in
all ways forgiven.

II.

Momentous breath
breath so simple
such simple breath
breath momentous.
In this moment's peace
this moment's grace
nurturing breath…
nourishing breath.

Break Time

Maybe you've lost
your patience
with your country
with a loved one
with yourself.
Maybe you've lost
your temper
at your gender at your species
at friends at strangers
or especially at yourself.

Maybe you've become too tightly wound
too judgmental
don't have Zen spirit
at least not when it counts.
Maybe you're constipated
or maybe you were raised Catholic
took it seriously... way too seriously
loved it loved it loved it all
until it all
fell like a ton of Baltimore catechisms
from a tower of incense-scented hocus-pocus gibber jabber.

Maybe you've been traumatized over seventy years
by all you've suffered
& by all the suffering you've inflicted on others
never thinking
you could or would.
Maybe you should take a breather
— a deep clean cleansing breath... take another... another...
keep breathing-breathing deeply-deeply
give yourself a break... before you break
 down... or in half... or in pieces.
Unwind. Judge not. Do compassion
including & especially self compassion
especially when such compassion appears undoable.
You know, it's been said
appearances can be deceiving.

Security Guard Working Graveyard Shift at Your Memory Museum

Wow, look at all this — all this amazing... *stuff*:
Clear clean crisp painful pleasurable
high-def memories & memories flawed fuzzy fizzy fluid flexible
from documented evidence to imaginative interpretation
from investigative journalism to creative nonfiction
from picaresque skits & sketches picaresque or Picasso-esque
to provocative sights evocative smells & hard-to-hear sounds
from flash fiction & hard-to-bear trash
to let's-get-lost labyrinths & mythologies
as bizarre & beguiling as those of the ageless Ancients.

Memories magnificent mean & meaningless
memories monumental microscopic everything in between
Quasimodo bell-ringing memories stored carefully carelessly
in a great gray brain-encased cranial vault guarded
by yours truly your fanatically loyal armed-to-the-teeth security guard
often making memories impregnable but just as often easily accessible
just flash fistfuls of cash & photo I.D. & not-so-secret salute
to unlock any & all after all
with these weapons obsolete & these bullets blanks
this poor ailing aging sentimental sentinel can be bribed.

Bootstraps

Next time some self-regarding self-described self-made
person
asserts their having pulled themselves up by their bootstraps
without fear nor favor
all by their righteous selves
through dint of nothing but their own
wits & will & sweat-stained work ethic,
demand to know (or politely inquire):

Where did these bootstraps come from?
Were they given? A gift?
Inherited? Stolen?
Did someone else make them and someone else simply sell them to you?
If you made the bootstraps yourself, who taught you how to do it?
Did you take a bootstrap-making class at a community college?
Did you view a how-to YouTube video?
Who made the video?

Did you slaughter an animal to make genuine leather bootstraps?
Did you then personally engage in the leather making?
Who taught you how to make leather?
Did you dispose of the leather-making waste responsibly?
Not much point to bootstraps without boots; so, where did the boots come from?
Hmm. Remind us again.
What, exactly, have you done solo?
Exactly.

Wannabe Handyman

Handyman kind of man you wish you were but aren't
never were never will be never ever heard the call.
Whether workaday pro or weekend warrior
admiration mixes with envy as naturally as hammer & nail
for man who builds swing set & jungle gym for grandchild lickety-split
man who plugs leaks tunes engines remodels bathrooms kitchens
man who never met do-it-yourself project he doesn't fall in love with.
Good man, honest modest reliable hardworking kindhearted bedrock blue-collar
humble-but-proud to show before & after images evidence of vision & skills
to turn useless ugly rubble wreckage or what was once big fat nothing
into something fixed up spruced up needed wanted useful
maybe even beautiful.

Handyman, which isn't to exclude women, no ma'am.
You've known many women every bit as handy as handiest of men
including two exes who could build backyard fences & treetop owl houses solo
& feel as at home in Home Depot as you'd feel orphaned
exes who could decipher poorly written repair manuals with skills of U.N. translators
while you shuddered with shameful impotent illiteracy lucky to know
how to light pilot or find main water valve.
But you're a man, damn it, you grew up in age when men were men
expected to be handymen not poets although theoretically two aren't mutually exclusive
but let's face it: back in the day men who did both weren't men
they were gods
either that or fairy godfathers.

It's not that you're still haunted daunted
by that rusty ethos at ripe age of seventy
& it's not that one's handyman IQ renders gender ID
but you kind of are & it sort of does.
Handyman, you admire envy each & every man who so naturally patiently
tinkers endlessly until thing's just right
man who inspects respects tools knows tools expertly
intimately
like singers know notes, like techies know codes
like poets know language like lovers know each other's flesh.

You're not one of those men you're not handy, man.
Never were never will be never got the call.

Rumble, Old Man, Rumble

"Float like a butterfly, sting like a bee! Rumble, young man, rumble!"
— Cassius Clay (before molding himself into Muhammad Ali) bellowing in unison with court jester/cheerleader Drew Bundini Brown, while training for his first title fight, in 1964.

And now, live! From inside your mind, some seventy years in the making, the moment of truth. Main event in the evening… of your life —
The Fight of a Lifetime!

In this corner, from the fabled land of spirit-nourishing stone-cold sobriety, wearing spine-straight heart-healthy optimism of believing it's not too late to make profound personal change…

Introducing the late-blooming proverbial overnight success who arrived on this planet some 26,000 overnights ago,
(stretching *fr* sound as if it were salt-water taffy)… Frrrreedom Frrrrom!.

And in this corner, wearing know-it-all cynicism & dead-eyed Darwinian survival skills, desultory champ for decades of decadence, weighing in with chump's usual baggage of guilt and shame, but also shrewd pluck and dumb luck…

from deep in the heart of long-buried traumas
(rolling the r with the flair of Orson Welles channeling P.T. Barnum)
— Frrreeedom To! Bell rings. Sounds like Reveille. Or Ravel. Bolero?

Freedom To looms like Harm, in the way. But Freedom From comes ready to rock and roll, unafraid knowing he might get hurt, get knocked on his ass, but he's prepared to get up, bob and weave, stick and move, rope-a-dope.

Freedom To goes for the KO. Freedom to steal, cheat, lie, get high, sink low, fuck around & fuck up. Freedom From counter-punches floating like a butterfly stinging like a bee — formula made famous by Cassius lean and hungry.

Freedom From finds his rhythm free and easy, freedom from righteous indignation, from revenge, from anti-social media, from angry haunting pasts, paranoid daunting futures, from addled consciousness, from deceit, including especially self-deceit, from self itself

Freedom To throws slow aimless punches at air hot with rot.
Freedom From digs in, cheers up, hears hoary exhortation enlivened, enriched, transformed, infused with timely twist: Rumble, old man, rumble!

Vanity Unfair

Chapter 1: Childhood

Too small, too weak, too shy,
too... well... childish,
believing in Santa & Jesus
& Pledge of Allegiance
& professional rasslin' on TV
far too much for far too long.

Chapter 2: Adolescence

Teeth full of braces, face full of zits,
plump, pointy, puss-filled pizza-face zits.
Too skinny, too tall, too lazy, too cowardly
to fend off bullies, to express sexuality.
Too conflicted, too, attracted to
philosophies of the pope & Playboy magazine

Chapter 3: Adulthood

Able to pass for normal at last,
future is now, what's past is past.
Teeth straight, complexion clear, muscles toned,
weight in sync with height,
shyness out, hedonism in, sexuality expressed
alas & alack, careless & faithless.

Chapter 4: Golden years and beyond

Bald scalp, blurred vision,
turkey neck, prune face,
achy hips, slower streams of piss,
arteries hardening, erections softening,
heartburn, heartache,
irritable bowel, irritable soul.

Epilogue

Oh vanity so foul, oh vanity unfair
& still whining after all these years.

Hush, Memory

No need to remember your father getting caught shoplifting
when you were thirteen which would have made him forty.
No need to remember your own thieving years —
beer and smokes at seventeen while supermarket stock boy
company car at eighteen while newspaper copy boy,
cash at nineteen cheating pals playing poker,
no need to remember your indelicate delinquent days, no need at all.

No need to remember playing with matches at age nine
burning weedy-junky-trashy urban lot
watching winking flames & stone-faced firefighters do their jobs
no need to remember getting molested at fourteen on the subway
no need to remember confused conflicted feelings
toward unpopular boy in your all-boys Catholic high school
no need to remember failing to protect younger brother from bullies.

No need to remember flunking tryouts for school ball teams
or your adolescent acne looking like moldy strawberry fields forever
no need to remember dead-eyed teen neighbor who teed off
slapping you silly & years later your mother telling you she saw
whole thing from kitchen window but stayed mum
no need to remember leaving one lover cold — *snap!* — just like that
another leaving you pathetic you boo-hoo you blubbering.

No need to excavate deep-buried memories
as if you're a miner laboring in dark dank tunnels of your mind
no need to ask your memory to speak
— you're no Nabokov writing celebrated sophisticated memoir
your memory requires no request no urging
your manic memory never stops digging discovering
hush memory — your memory needs to hush.
Your memory needs to shut the fuck up.

Will the Real You Please Stand Up

Gentle lovers exploited,
faithful spouses abandoned,
daughter & son cast aside.

Brothers, buddies all betrayed,
father, mother afterthought.
Deny, ignore, justify.

Break hearts, crush souls, lust, leave, weave
shift blame/shame into nostalgia,
spin sins into sentimental sediment.

Lie, cheat, play games sadistic.
Pose, obsess masochistic.
Get high, get laid, X-rated, ex-Catholic.

Revise, remake, cut and paste.
Go numb, hide out, hunker down.
Screw up, pump up, cover up.

Scared, scarred, sow, reap dank dark bloom.
Sleep, dream, sleep-walk wake, cringe, crawl, creep.
Waste time. Bide time. Time … it runs out.

Nor Was He The Marlboro Man

Father & son at Yankee Stadium
to celebrate the son turning thirteen
at Yankee Stadium not to see the Yankees
but to see the football Giants
which is what New Yorkers still called those Giants
to distinguish them from the baseball Giants
even though those baseball Giants had abandoned New York for San Francisco
three long seasons ago.

Father & son
at Yankee Stadium
to see the football Giants — *their* Giants
the son disappointed, crushed really, to learn his hero Charlie Conerly
nursing an injury from the previous week's heroics
wouldn't quarterback the team this day

— the father secretly joyous shamefully jealous of Conerly
with whom he shared a birth year but nothing else
nothing a teenage son would find heroic.
Unlike Conerly
the father wasn't the Giants quarterback
nor was he the Marlboro Man.

Father & son
at Yankee Stadium
the father sad, shocked really, to see *his* hero Frank Gifford
tackled so cruelly so violently
Gifford's blue helmeted head bouncing
like a dribbled basketball on the street-tough turf
the vision of Gifford's beautiful body carried off on a stretcher
providing a blinding flashback to luckless friends on Luzon f
ifteen short years earlier

— the son shamefully joyous secretly jealous
of Gifford's toughness & movie-star looks
jealous of Gifford's gridiron grace Gifford's ability to inspire
awe & admiration & actual cheerleader cheers & tears from the father
— nothing a scrawny awkward buck-toothed bookworm teenager
could ever hope to inspire.

Accident on the L.I.E.

They're just cruising keeping pace
with all those cars ahead on the Long Island Expressway
going 60-70-80 miles per hour
a couple of 22-year-olds
leaving their families' old city
heading toward their newly adopted old city
in a not-that-old forest-green '65 Mustang
in the first hour of a four-hour drive
as the sun sets
on their first Thanksgiving weekend
as a married couple.

Siamese cats in the back in their cages
wailing away another day of traveling discontent.
Wife in the passenger seat already dozing already oblivious.
They're just cruising
keeping pace with all those cars ahead…

When two moments' distractions
two what-might've-been daydreams
slam head-on into each other —
football on the radio
Namath injured? Season ruined?…
and then recalling earlier-in-the-day shock
disguised as friendly surprise
when ex-girlfriend girl-next-door dropped by
just to say hi and bye…

No longer going 60-70-80…
all those cars ahead stopped instead
the Long Island Expressway
transformed into instant parking lot…
All those cars aren't moving
but still rushing toward them
coming closer-closer-closer
— how's that possible?

Will they die?

Hitting the brakes,
slamming hard hard pressing down hard on the brakes
needing to stop more than the Mustang
but no matter
those cars ahead still
coming closer-closer-closer...

Will they die?

Slowing down some but not stopping — no, far from stopping
sudden surreal sound of metal smashing,
glass breaking, steam hissing, steering useless
the whole kaleidoscopic scene
simultaneously fast-forward and slo-mo
it's a movie — no it's real too damn real
veering sliding turning spinning skidding crashing
as if on ice but there's no ice
this Thanksgiving weekend has been unseasonably mild
— one might say deceitfully mild.

Sudden-stop-sudden-silence.

Did they die?

Splish-Splash

You run a hot bath
its fog enveloping you in steamy affection
you liberally... indulgently... sprinkle in
metaphysical crystals of appreciation
— for what? — doesn't matter
think of something
think of anything
just don't overthink
gotta know when to say when
regarding thinking over-thinking
— don't overthink and drive
— don't over-think and bathe, neither.

You marvel at the
unaccountably big
uncountable soapy bubbles — beautifully
transforming a bath — beautifully
transporting a bath
into a launch...
into Inner Space.

You get in get into it... get all the way into it...
 Immerse yourself...
Luxuriate in the nourishing nurturing warmth
of unclouded affectionate appreciation...
... you give yourself permission to give yourself space...
to space out.

You soak... sit & space & soak...
until the air cools and the water chills
until the bubbles burst
as the water and the air and the bubbles certainly inevitably will

but no matter...
you've soaked up all that good-will warmth...
... all that affectionate appreciation.

You're good to go back & give back...

back to Reality... rotating Reality... revolving evolving Reality...
— at least for the next twenty-four hours...
you're good to go!

Giving Thanks to Your Trash Collectors

Carefully gather your stash of trash your shame & blame
& dusty disappointments from all the rooms & broom closets
where you've lived all your lives all these years...
all the nooks & crannies in your palaces of fine arts
(and the not-so-fine less-than-palatial places, too)
and in the crude oil refineries of your spilled mess of memory.

Securely place all your carefully gathered trash in a bin
(but you might need something bigger,
maybe a roomy dumpster of your own)
while turning your head
away from the decaying odor
of the fraying paralyzing past.

Stuff in today's anger & angst
as if they're mold-laden leftovers
from last year's Thanksgiving
along with rotten uprooted regrets
& add the untamed unmuzzled barking fear
of failures & futures near & far.

Close lid tightly... but not too tightly.
Mustn't ever close these things too tightly
or else the toxic gaseous pressure
builds & builds & builds & builds
until there's an explosion — or implosion —
until someone loses a tooth or an eye... or two.

Give an unwavering wave of thanks to the collectors of your trash
— stoic heroic essential workers, indeed —
when they drive up masked in their
huffing-puffing-farting brake-squealing trucks
when their truck's robotic monster arms
bear-hug your trash like a 'roid-raged kidnapper.

Don't merely meekly wave goodbye

to your freshly mashed trash driven away
far away (who really knows or cares where?)
But boldly bid Good Riddance — what a rush!
You feel like an adrenaline-amped extreme surfer
riding high on oceanic giants toward a lost paradise found anew.

What We Talk About When We Talk About Coffee

Never fails...

Coffee

first sip / first gulp
first thing / early / in the morning

sip if we've / slept the sleep
of innocence
gulp if go get 'em's / our day's go-to.

Coffee
beans / purchased / selected / carefully / organic
shade grown / fair trade
full bodied / dark roast
French.

Coffee
shiny black beans
we grind
so precisely / lovingly hover / over which
seductively / we patiently pour
just-boiled / meticulously measured
filtered water.

Coffee
shiny black beans
nestled in / non-bleached / eco-friendly filter
yielding / yielding / gently consenting...

Coffee
residing royally / in sweet spot / between
hotter / much hotter / than lukewarm
but not as hot / not nearly as hot
as piping hot.

Never fails
—
first sip / first gulp / first thing / early morning
coffee
tastes / delightful /decadent /delicious
exquisitely so / energizing /satisfying /comforting / sensual
miraculous moment / lingers like / well-groomed beggar
then flees / like / wrongly accused / fugitive.

Coffee
Always fails / to recapture / moment / feeling
from that first sip / first gulp ...
first thing / early morning
no matter how / many more / more & more
sips or gulps / cups or mugs
it leave us / far from / satisfaction's / shores
instead
we're left / all jittery all day / all day / all jingly-jangly.

Always fails / always fails
think / we'd stop
after first / sip / or gulp
think / we'd be better
at enjoying embracing / first sip / first gulp
afterglow
then stop / needing speeding /caffeine fiend fixing
obsessing / over / recapturing
vanished / magical moment
and instead / mourn / honorably mourn it's
passing.

But we don't
stop.
Don't stop slipping
sipping.
Don't stop grinding
gulping.

We never stop. / We never learn.
We never ...
stop.

Clocks Striking Thirteen on a Bright Cold Day

Time, it marches it routs like armies invading
it conquers it prances marauding parading.

Time, it flees it stretches infinitely beyond
leaving us our world definitively behind.

Time, elusive it flits it flutters it flies
like sapho satyr saturn blue butterflies.

No wonder Nabokov obsessed
hunted captured pinned them possessed.

Forgiven

You're innocent
I'm innocent

We're all innocent
but innocent of what?

I deserve this.
I don't deserve that.

You deserve that.
You don't deserve this.

We deserve this.
We don't deserve that.

They deserve all of that.
They don't deserve any of this.

But here's the thing about deserve:
Deserve's got nothing to do with anything.

Dreaming & Dancing

Dreaming at dusk
when eyes soften
the shape-shifting night
you seek to climb
higher truer
self-reflection
of dancing at dawn
with your sins
& your secrets.

Poking Sharp Stick Into Insidious Eye — It's About Time

insidious eye idiot box boob tube
—high school teacher's elitist
conceited critique of TV circa
1963

we conceded his point but point
proves moot, conceding TV's voodoo
to attract distract mesmerize anesthetize

seduce with eyewitness news hope horror
JFK elected inaugurated assassinated,
even witnessing assassin assassinated

boob tube, idiot box, its unblinking
insidious eye high tech narcotic
but what were poor addicts to do?

from fetishized flag waving
propagandized war mongering
to Fox News scoundrels' raging bull

from Flintstones to Simpsons cartoons
Alan Shepard teeing off on the moon
to loony Tricky Dick's quitting befitting

first TV generation we've gone
from 12-inch black-and-white images
as snowy as Christmas in Saskatoon

to today's Best Buy hi-def deities
like private theater sound and screens
to watch cops docs sit-coms stand-ups

mobsters mad men masterpieces
on Petroleum Broadcasting Service
WrestleMania celebrity megalomania

nine innings two halves four quarters
overtime all the time promotion
of conspicuous compliant consumption

endless ads for painless perfections
of body mind vanity insanity
even soft-core ads for erections

enough no more why now?
now or never it's about time
time's all it's ever been about

talk show pablum Orwellian reality
canned laughs conned public
so many channels so little reflection

enough no more what took so long?
oh just usual predictable inexcusable
excuses explanations rationalizations

America's got talent for short attention
with pox of pundits morbid mantra
if it bleeds it leads breaking news broken

enough is enough is enough already
more than enough staring bingeing
cringing cheering leering loathing

enough no more it's about time
no longer fat and forever
now thinning ticking bomb

now offering late-blooming balm
calmly rejecting insidious eye's
ire enough no more it's about time

when enough is more than enough
when brain-saving no-brainer no time
like now turn off pull plug disconnect

reconnect to outside world inside you
overdue to poke sharp stick into insidious
eye aspire to channel better angels

gave it up for Lent as 12 year old
giving it up for good as 70 year old
healing freeing feeling wholly healthy.

Mourning Doves
& Morning Gunshots

Sounding like drought-dry branches crackling in a campfire
seven rapid gunshots mute mourning doves' morning cooing
as sweet/troubled sixteen-year-old
Jeremiah
artistically inclined Jeremiah
sole person of color in family of four
Living
in nearly all-white ultra-progressive small town
math tutor to classmates Jeremiah
Breathing
mild March morning air
for months slowly steadily losing grip
on so-called reality
suddenly locked in so-cold
vise grip of psychotic episode
Shot dead
crack-crackcrack-crackcrackcrack-crack
by two deputies threatened
by pocket knife Jeremiah wields
inside family van parked
in driveway of family rural home
while summoned ambulance idles nearby
as if lulled by laguna's enveloping fog
with mother adoptive father younger half-brother
having called for help expecting
Help
instead witnessing hell experiencing hell
intimate torturous
Hell
in all its no-exit permanence.

Meanwhile...

mourning doves
in shock perhaps or
out of respect maybe or
in protest possibly impossibly stay mute
all next morning too.

— *for Jeremiah Chass, killed by Sonoma County Sheriff's deputies John Misita and James Ryan, March 12, 2007, in unincorporated Sebastopol, California.*

Last Love Last

Ashes-and-dust doom looms
as planet gets hotter
drought gets drier
polar ice melts
seas and political poisons rise
air foul from forests ablaze
flames of willful ignorance scorching
everyone everywhere...

And yet... and yet...
in these our so-called golden years
on a clear clean gilded summer afternoon
somehow we're emboldened
to make rest-of-our-life commitments
lovers' lovely vows
no matter challenges
personal or planetary.

Last love last.

When we look into each other's eyes
we intend to see
the best versions of ourselves:
each vulnerable
each the other's champion
each the other's defender.
We intend to look — really look
into each other's eyes...

Offering passion and kindness
playfulness
and good humor
devotion
and steadfast emotional security
patience
and forgiveness
... always forgiveness.

Last love last.

A Kiss at the Corner of 19th & Holloway

They kiss chastely — mere pecks on the cheek —
whenever driving past San Francisco State University
at the corner of 19th Avenue & Holloway
— a kiss recalling two platonic years as classmates
when each discovered the other saw in the other
something lively & lovely & left it at that
— a kiss also saluting twenty more platonic years
witnessing each other's weddings each other's children growing.

It's also a kiss grieving another twenty years
of having lost contact or of having
allowed contact to be lost or at least misplaced
like an old moldy copy of the campus newspaper
featuring their fast-fading side-by-side bylines
real-life daily life having a willfully blind
lazy mazy life of its own along with
that astronomical ninety-nine-mile separation.

Mostly, though, it's a private joyful shy kiss as they drive
past SF State at the corner of 19th & Holloway
celebrating the unlikely *what-were-the-odds!?*
reuniting & remarkably rediscovering each other
in a quiet quite late-in-life lottery-luck passion
with which they've replaced platonic with erotic
& where commitment & contentment caress
like sunsets' burnt sienna glow upon Mt. Tam's peak.

Reflections & Refractions at Bodega Bay

Undulating with merciless mystery
midnight-clear blue Bodega Bay
in late October reflects & refracts
high noon's burning bright Vitamin D-rich rays...

Glistening
like beads of celestial sweat
Twinkling
like night sky-studded stars
Blinking
like *Close Encounters'*
cosmos-crossing ships
carrying other-worldly peace-seeking sojourners...

and I look & gawk in awe I gaze & gape
wrapped in the cool calm
of a salty autumnal sea-breeze balm
until angst creases my brow yet again seizes my soul...

as I wonder
Why
I'm here...
 as I worry
Why
you're there...
miles & miles & miles & miles away
— landlocked.

Facelift

In midst of daunting divorce she never saw coming
she painfully painstakingly excises her face
glowing smiling from extended family photo
that doesn't include her clan of no-shows
taken at in-laws' fiftieth anniversary
celebrating other mother other father
who love her as if she were their daughter
unlike pill-popping papa who long ago
smacks her face calls her stupid
or rum-soaked mum as clueless cupid
pushing her child's mask-of-makeup face on dates
at barely thirteen with older boys hardly boys hardly harmless.

Rage resentment over family history
of being cut out left out thrown out
flash back with shock of electric cruel current
in midst of daunting divorce she never saw coming
she painfully painstakingly severs ties sends
face-lifted photo to that other mother other father.

Unhappily Happy

All progress is change
but all change isn't progress...

So she stares at the stern-faced soft-eyed reflection in the mirror
& she sees a glassy portrait of her grandmotherly-looking mother
who would be ninety-nine now if she'd lived another six years
her firm but fair mother
her mother forever faithful to her father
her mother who stares back at her forlorn prodigal firstborn
& wonders & worries about this latest change
this latest heartbreak breakup breakdown
so stark & sudden
so stressful & unsought
this latest in a lengthy list
of late-life laments
& she doesn't ask

Aren't you too old for this shit?

Which would be to the point
but a point too sharp too hurtful too out of character
so instead so wise & tender her mother asks:

Is this change from a happily unhappy
old woman busy-busy with a needy-needy
big-hearted but brain-pained mate
to an unhappily happy old woman alone
with her freedom to create whatever whenever
alone with her oh-so precious peace of mind
although a piece might be missing...
Is this change (forced as it was) progress?
Or is it simple brutal adapt-or-die change?
If this change isn't progress,
will this change swallow you? Or spare you?

She looks at the face in the mirror
she seeks her fate in the mirror.

UFO Abduction

Rotting rustic termite-teeming
rural bungalow high on wine
country hill
wasn't without its charms
it's why this man & this woman fell in languorous love with it
as clueless as they'd fallen in love with each other
or had fallen in love with potent notion of falling in love with love
of free-falling falling free

in late middle age
leaving former lives
too weighty to be taken on this latest fanciful flight
this selfish journey of self-discovery
falling in lulling dulling love
with views of sun-dappled vineyards
& flash-flooding Laguna de Santa Rosa's flying
buzzing creeping crawling swampy primal life

fallen for location location location
privacy primary
& promise of cheap rent — well, affordable, anyway
until sudden singular lives broke in
like some home invasion
broke up couple's co-habited habitat
couple seized in uncharted seas
of sudden retirement

with born-again stranger singular lives
what once permeated permanence
crashed head-on slashed
seventeen long loving years
that flirted with forever
into seventeen short never-mind years
gone without a trace
like a UFO abduction.

Arrow Stuck in Neck

Strangest most surreal of all those creatures
who lived in & around the rented bungalow on that wine country hill — stranger
than the long-married human couple gradually suddenly
turning from intimates to strangers —
there crouches an eyes-a-poppin' tail-a-twitchin' squirrel
looking perfectly normal in its natural environment
in its unnerving unnatural alarming circumstance
as if subject of slapstick or object
of small-minded hunter's small-game aim
— an arrow sticking through its narrow neck.

He (whispering):
You've gotta see this it's unbelievable
it's sick sordid strange
come quick now look oh my god look
at that pitiful creature who should be in agony
but doesn't seem to know it
at that critter who should be dead
but clearly isn't.

But she's too late. Doesn't see.
Doesn't really believe without having seen.

It was there, he swears,
but now it's gone.

As were they soon enough
the long-married human couple gone
separate ways after nearly twenty years
amicably tearfully finally.
She
done with exhaustive experiments in domesticity.
He
in further want desperate need of home improvement.

Crawlspace

Rosters of rodents
bide their time
scratching screeching
from within
crawlspace in hallway
above & in-between
long-married couple's
wine country bungalow bedrooms.
Rosters of rodents
disappear reappear disappear
for weeks or months
or years at a time it seems.

But rodents reappear
this time no doubt
finally having come to stay
to live & die
holding hell-raising all-night Irish wakes
& making Olympic-like mad dashes down
long-married couple's
afraid-to-leave afraid-to-stay
frayed closeted clothing hanging like executed prisoners
in separate bedrooms bedrooms separated
by sickly sweet death-scented crawlspace.

On Either Side of Broad Bay Window

Soothing sights
of big bright yellow green red blue black birds
bathing
in stone backyard birdbath
in early autumn evening
after hard day
soaring
& singing ballads or protest songs or national anthems
except
for those that crashed concussed
into bungalow's broad bay wine country window
beyond restorative recipes of Bird Rescue's best.

While on other side
of bungalow's broad bay wine country window…

Unsettling sights
of a swan-necked glass-beaded bong
uniting
with wine bottles
uniting
with beer bottles
uniting
with whiskey bottles
recruiting
a couple
of laughing lusting stoned silly sullen drunken
restless roguish
friendly-fire-wounded
armies of one.

Owl House

From her long lived-in rented
weathered wine country home
high on her haunted hill...
From her attic's airless claustrophobic clutter

— everything from scrapbooks in scrapheaps
to unhelpful self-help guides & sauce-stained cookbooks
from used toys abused or merely toyed with lifetimes ago
to *passe* political posters (*Run Jesse Run!*)
from camping gear with torn tents
from within which smuggled ex-lovers snuggled
high in the Sierra or below
sea level in the springtime bloom of Death Valley —

a fragile fearless wise & wary woman
tumbles into air autumnal
to craft to labor with handsome hands strong & skilled
creased with dusty history & grimy geography
a neat clean simple wholesome home
for the winged predator rarely heard & never seen
& mounts this neat clean simple wholesome home high
high on her haunted hill.

When Dying Deer Appeared

Sweltering summer when dying deer
appeared as if posed frozen in seedy
weedy gopher-holed drought-ravaged backyard
yet still somehow evoked visions
of beastly beauty & deep dignity

they might've tensed sensed
from kitchen window
watched by aging boomer couple's
tame eyes squinting
framing their wild eyes haunting

witnessing ribs poking through taut flesh
like samurai swords under dirty dun-colored linen
beautiful beastly bodies transcending art
descending delicately into decay
yet spirits vigilant. Patient.

No illusions delusions
unlike human couple together
safe secure thriving
conniving desiring
dreams apart.

Burning Coals & Hothouse Flowers

She's right. He doesn't know
what it's like
to be a recovering addict
wrestling or karate-kicking
or just holding a high-stakes staring contest
with recovering
every day
taking depressing doses of meds
every day
carrying scary psychic scars
every day
shedding self defense always doing for others
spreading oneself so thin
exposing thinnest of skin.

She's right. He doesn't know what any of that's like.
But he does know what's it's like

to live with such a person

to love such a person
to be in love
with such a person — another sort of addiction itself.

It's like walking barefoot on eggshells
scattered over broken glass
strewn over burning coals
surrounded by fields of hothouse flowers
so fragile
they release paralyzing pollen
if he sneezes on them
or if a chill breeze breathes on them
or if he glances askance at them
while searching scrambling scuffling
desperate... oh so desperate
for a deal... any deal
on insurance — the no-fault kind.

Road to Recovery

After sixty days alone
tomorrow he'll drive sixty miles
to greet his lover masked
bring her home after her sixty days
of 12-step recovery
(this time it'll stick, right?)
after his sixty days of 3-step recovery
of his sense of calm & order & self-worth.

Eager to recover their intimacy
their inside jokes
their outsized yokes
of needs & wants
supply & demand
they'll hope for the best
 they'll brace for the tests
 each day each will take.

Tomorrow he'll drive sixty miles
to recover his lover unmasked
but tonight he'll sleep & dream
on her side not on his side
& wear not his sweatshirt sleepwear
but her bright pure white camisole
so soft & snug so safe & secure
against his beat-skipping heart.

Mother Knew Best

Your father being a glass-half-full type
& lead cheerleader for all three of his sons
— the straight one, the gay one & you — the California one —
cheerily chided 'Well, third time's a charm!'

thirteen years ago when you were fifty-nine
& told your eighty-five year-old parents
(who'd been wedlocked to each other sixty years)
that you were committing matrimony yet again.

But your mother knowing you her firstborn all too well
gave a different sort of sardonic pep talk
more like a finger-wagging warning:
'Ok, but three strikes you're out!'

Turns out mother knew best — no surprise there
but their cute clever comical words of comfort & caution
in retrospect ring wrong unkind unwise
keeping count to reward winners & label losers

as if longevity alone proves anything
other than marathoners' skills to abide
as if sprinters & milers don't also run
some splendid grueling satisfying races of their own

as if hundred-meter dash is somehow less
for its dash of excitement
its flash of extinction
as if all the so-called winners

& all the also-rans
aren't crying
grateful bitter tears...
together... at the finish line.

Catawampus

When you're the one who leaves
you're a conscience-scrubbed surgeon (or cold-blooded butcher)
you're calm & capable running a complete con
you're a self-serving peace-loving war monger
when you're the one who leaves
you're a smug bonfire-building book-burning thug
muddying memories, rewriting history
fierce savage destructive
you're Employee of the Month at Orwell's Ministry of Truth
when you're the one who leaves
you rip out the rear-view mirror
you stomp on the accelerator
you're a regular bat out of hell
infamy incarnate *persona non grata*
when you're the one who leaves.

When you're the one who's been left
you're left lonely angry anemic
unable to grip cold hard truth
only righteous regret
self-respect so suspect
there's no food no sleep no break
from pathetic plunge
into all-day all-night pity parties
when you're the one who's been left
it's devastating enervating humiliating
it's earthquake tornado volcano fiasco
you're askew awry victim chump uncool fool
when you're the one who's been left
you're cast in rejected roles in surreal scenes
of grand opera comic opera (but mostly) soap opera.

Best Friends & Devoted Lovers

In the beginning
so many red flags
it could've been May Day in Moscow:
His guilt, her exes, her guilt, his exes
her snoring, his jealousy, his sneering, her jealousy
her depression, his impatience
her son, his daughter, her dog, his cat
the bottle-a-night wine drinking
& their pretty-pretty-good-but-something's-missing sex.

In the beginning
could they see all those flags
through the shimmering spectacle
through the raw red-blooded blizzard?

Of course they did but they saw them
not as warnings but as bullfighters' capes
& they'd get high on the adrenaline rush
of flamboyantly twirling one red cape after another
provoking seducing the demonic beasts
confident in each other's ability to stick 'em & slay 'em
slay 'em all, cut off their ears, castrate them.

Or did they see all those red flags
as the fiery bright eternal flames
of their midlife revolutionary romantic parade?
Yippee-hooray for red flags!
Let's wave 'em like crazy, wave the fuck out of them!
Laugh in the flags' red faces until their own faces turned blue.

After all, they were best friends & devoted lovers
& they would transcend the red flags
or so they truly believed
rise above high above all those red flags
with work & play & sobriety & creativity
with hikes in the forests & strolls on the beaches
with warm smiles & belly laughter
including laughter at themselves.

But the years the sneaky sadistic years
taking their damn sweet time
doing their dirty nasty work gradually suddenly
and one day it's indeed May Day
as in "May Day! May Day! May Day!"
Life-or-death cries for rescue or escape
the parades & pageantry over
the *plaza de toros* trashed beyond recognition
the laughter and lovemaking
having given way
to binge drinking & neck-deep debt
& furtive pot smoking & pill popping
and a brief affair and a not-so-brief affair
& the depression not budging not giving way at all
& the amazing colossal jealousies
& a panic attack leading to a night in the ER
& estrangements from children
who weren't children anymore
& the incredible shrinking empathy
unhappiness relentlessly eroding happiness
like sneaker waves crashing into a moonscape
& it's all desperately needing to be cleared away
like so many tons of confetti
fit for neither compost nor recycling.

Fact Checker's Notes (1996)

Local rag's four-inch murder-suicide story
with itty-bitty 18-point headline
Two Bodies Found
gets victim's age wrong, misspells first name.
She was 41, not 42.
Wasn't Katherine with "e" in middle,
was Katharine with "a" in middle.
Like Hepburn.
Known as Kate, also like Hepburn.
And equally compelling in roles she played:
youth gymnast,
college art student who adored Toulouse-Lautrec and Hieronymus Bosch,
morose gut-laughing stoner,
daughter of divorce,
jealous of science brainiac big sister,
pregnant at 17 by 24-year-old formerly platonic boyfriend
who followed her from Boston to Berkeley.
But *Two Bodies Found* has none of that.

Two Bodies Found says Kate worked as a waitress;
but omits her being a film aficionado,
her favorites:
the blissfully naive *King of Hearts*
& *The Servant*, a piece of noir psycho-sexual nastiness.

No mention of pop song she liked to lip sync,
the impossibly ironic *I Can See Clearly Now*.
Or that she devoured Vonnegut's dark humor,
idolized the ballet of both Baryshnikov and Bruce Lee,
delighted in reading aloud *Phantom Toll Booth*
& smelled of tobacco & patchouli & cannabis sativa.

Two Bodies Found says Kate had husband (separated),
two sons (ages 10, 14),
but nothing about newborn girl she and formerly platonic boyfriend
gave up for adoption.
Mother, daughter met once, 22 years later,
on intense day of hugging, mutual crying.

After that day, solo crying.

Killer's name Marsh, real whack job.
Was he 44 or 45? Who cares?
Knew Kate for year, little longer maybe. That doesn't matter, either.
Not to be found in *Two Bodies Found*,
police say — off the record —
Marsh smoked a cigarette after shooting Kate in the chest, twice,
before lying beside her and shooting himself in the chest. Once.

Whack job's mother spins it as double suicide
— Romeo & Juliet
or some shit.
It wasn't.

Postgame Wrap

He's the kind of person
who after a selfish-selfless inner tug of war
gives her his prized well-insulated
San Francisco Giants windbreaker
because he's got another windbreaker
(no team logo but just as good)
and she's got none and they'll be sitting
in the bleachers and it likely will get cold & windy
around the seventh-inning stretch
even colder & windier on the postgame walk
 about a mile long along the Embarcadero
from the ballpark to the Larkspur ferry.

She's the kind of person
who gives her recently received
well-insulated Giants windbreaker
to the shivering sleeveless homeless man
she sees curled up like a fetus
along the Embarcadero
during their postgame walk
from the ballpark to the Larkspur ferry
— the kind of person
who does such a thing instinctively
not thinking nor caring
about her own privileged comfort.

He's the kind of person
who clutches awkwardly at annoyance
& stubborn shameless resentment
like a bratty hyperactive child
at the Monterey Bay Aquarium
trying to grab hold of an eel.

She's the kind of person
who has as much use
for resentment & annoyance
as that eel does — the kind of person
who follows her big-hearted impulses...
and never looks back.

Unsolicited Advice to the Sorrow-Stricken

Fighting with Sorrow gets you nothing…
well, it'll get your ass kicked is what
fighting with Sorrow will get you.
And even then, Sorrow won't leave
even after it's kicked your ass
it'll stick around looking to kick your ass
again. And again. Sorrow's a sadist.
It'll never get bored kicking your ass.
Even if somehow you manage to kick Sorrow's ass
Sorrow's too proud too stubborn too stupid
to leave you alone because Sorrow is nothing
if not a masochist too oh yeah Sorrow won't leave
just because you bloodied its nose fattened its lip
blackened its eye kicked its ass. No way.
Fighting with Sorrow gets you nothing.

Debating with Sorrow gets you nowhere.
You can command the strategic logic
of a chess grandmaster or a philosopher's lucid locution
or electric elocution of a megachurch preacher
Sorrow won't care. Sorrow will just stare back
like a blank-eyed bovine with a sneaky sneer
etched at a corner of its thin bloodless lips
as if to say it doesn't matter how evolved you are or how righteous.
Sorrow doesn't care and Sorrow ain't leaving you alone.
Debating with Sorrow gets you nowhere.

Sitting with Sorrow… now you're getting somewhere.
What you've got to do with Sorrow is sit with it.
That's right. Just sit with it.
No fighting no biting no pushing no shoving
No talking arguing chit-chatting jibber-jabbering.
No trying to outsmart outfox Sorrow.
You sit with Sorrow…
until the chaotic roiling oppressive aggressive silence settles
 into something somewhat serene — perversely plain

ordinary garden-variety dime-a-dozen sadness, maybe.
Don't ask how long it'll take. It'll take as long as it takes.
Hey nobody said it would be easy. But it works.
Tried and true. Live and let live. Sit with it. Sit with Sorrow.
Respect Sorrow and Sorrow will respect you.

Supremacy

You're not a god but you play one on the TV
that's always on in your mind and you have a mind
filled with the adrenaline-fueled bloodlust of a big-game hunter
wielding almighty uptight Old Testament judgment
killing fat & lazy low-flying houseflies with tightly rolled-up
listings of unaffordable Bay Area real estate & rentals

and you wipe out countless invading anarchist ants
alternating sociopathic equanimity with the righteous rage
of a genocidal Crusader armed with vinegar-soaked rags
never wondering whether you're engaging in torture a little too enthusiastically
— you're not a god but it's a great guilty vainglorious pleasure
to play one on the TV that's always on in your mind

— the same TV that also shows you going to
remarkably merciful lengths to save spiders
— even the really big ugly hairy elusive speedy spiders —
patiently placing them in the backyard or on the front porch
channeling the loving-kindness taught to you years ago
by otherworldly Buddhist nuns living in placid Penngrove.

No you're not a god but you play one on the TV
that's always on in your cabled cobbled contradictory mind
with its hundreds (or is it thousands?) of channels
most of which rarely show anything worth watching
but still you find mindless comfort channel-surfing
your infinite godlike time away while mindfully agitated.

Remember the good old days when you were new
in the world and the TV always on in your mind
offered only three channels — one called Mommy another Daddy —
and those three channels were enough and there was no need
to channel surf because you never got bored never needed
to kill time nor anything else nor rescue anything neither?

Bone Marrow Biopsy Reverberations

The oncologist instructs you to lay face down
like you're going to get a massage
except you're not going to get a massage.

And you think of the thousands of dollars
you spent while hooked on erotic massage
during the final years of your third marriage.

The oncologist plunges a needle as long as your middle finger
into the base of your spine
and says it'll feel like a bee sting.

And you remember sixty summers ago
when you and both younger brothers
were stung by bees ... right between the eyes.

Was that the summer you failed to protect one of them
from bullies? Or was it the summer you misread the other's
raised-arm alarm for a vigorous swimming-hole hello?

You're told you're a good patient with a high pain tolerance
and you flash back to twelve years of Catholic schools and you think:
no — obedient & stoic with high tolerance for authority figures.

You're told you'll get the bone marrow biopsy results
in two weeks and you realize you've heard the word "marrow"
more times this month than in all your seventy-three years.

And you remember your mother telling you when you were a child:
eat your baked beans — they'll put marrow in your bones
and you had no idea if that were true ... or even what it meant.

Acknowledgements

The following poems, some of which are altered in content or title from what appears in this collection, were first published in the following journals:

Arrow Stuck in Neck, Crawlspace, DNA Samples, Facelift, Hush Memory, King for a Day, On Either Side of Broad Bay Window in **Raw Art Review**.

Bone Marrow Biopsy Reverberations, Break Time in **The Write Launch**.

Catawampus, Love in the Time of the Cuban Missile Crisis, A Septuagenarian Atheist Prays in **The Esthetic Apostle**.

Wrestling vs. Boxing in **Cathexis Northwest Press**.

Mother Knew Best in **Gravitas**.

Owl House in **Haunted Waters Press**.

UFO Abduction in **Forbidden Peak Press**.

Giving Thanks to Your Trash Collectors, Uncool Kid in **MacQueen's Quinterly**.

Robert Eugene Rubino is a retired newspaper copy editor and sports columnist who was 70 in 2018 when his first poem was published, "Septuagenarian Atheist Prays" (The Esthetic Apostle). Since then he has published prose and poetry in various print and online literary journals. In 2016, he received a Pushcart Prize nomination in creative nonfiction for "Spinning Shame Into Nostalgia" (Hippocampus). "Vanity Unfair and Other Poems" is his first poetry collection. He is also the author of "Aficionado" (Humming Word Press) and "Douglas KOs Tyson" (UnCollected Press).

Also Available from Cathexis Northwest Press:

Something To Cry About
by Robert Krantz

Suburban Hermeneutics
by Ian Cappelli

God's Love Is Very Busy
by David Seung

that one time we were almost people
by Christian Czaniecki

Fever Dream/Take Heart
by Valyntina Grenier

The Book of Night & Waking
by Clif Mason

Dead Birds of New Zealand
by Christian Czaniecki

The Weathering of Igneous Rockforms in High-Altitude Riparian Environments
by John Belk

If A Fish
by George Burns

How to Draw a Blank
by Collin Van Son

En Route
by Jesse Wolfe

sky bright psalms
by Temple Cone

Moonbird
by Henry G. Stanton

southern athiest. oh, honey
by d. e. fulford

Bruises, Birthmarks & Other Calamities
by Nadine Klassen

Wanted: Comedy, Addicts
by AR Dugan

They Curve Like Snakes
by David Alexander McFarland

the catalog of daily fears
by Beth Dufford

Shops Close Too Early
by Josh Feit

<u>Destructive Heresies</u>
by Milo E. Gorgevska

<u>Bodies of Separation</u>
by Chim Sher Ting

Cathexis Northwest Press

www.ingramcontent.com/pod-product-compliance
Lightning Source LLC
Chambersburg PA
CBHW030345100526
44592CB00010B/836